SCRIPTURE AND MYTH

*THE TYNDALE BIBLICAL THEOLOGY
LECTURE, 1956*

*The lecture was delivered at Tyndale House, Cambridge, on July 2nd, 1956 at a meeting convened by the Tyndale Fellowship for Biblical Research.*

# SCRIPTURE AND MYTH

## AN EXAMINATION OF RUDOLF BULTMANN'S PLEA FOR DEMYTHOLOGIZATION

By
PHILIP EDGCUMBE HUGHES
M.A., B.D., D.LITT.

WIPF & STOCK · Eugene, Oregon

Wipf and Stock Publishers
199 W 8th Ave, Suite 3
Eugene, OR 97401

Scripture and Myth
An Examination of Rudolf Bultmann's Plea for Demythologization
By Hughes, Philip E.
Copyright©1956 Inter-Varsity Press, UK
ISBN 13: 978-1-60899-126-6
Publication date 9/28/2009
Previously published by The Tyndale Press, 1956

This limited edition licensed by special permission of Inter-Varsity Press, UK.

# SCRIPTURE AND MYTH

## AN EXAMINATION OF RUDOLF BULTMANN'S PLEA FOR DEMYTHOLOGIZATION

IN recent years nothing has disturbed the serenity of the theological scene more than Professor Rudolf Bultmann's emphatic plea for the demythologization of the New Testament. Coming from a man of such reputation and undoubted ability as a New Testament scholar, this plea must be examined with all seriousness; indeed, there are, in my judgment, few religious thinkers of our day who have shown a deeper understanding and offered a more stimulating exegesis of the theology of the New Testament than has Rudolf Bultmann. But, at the same time, his writings provide us with a cogent reminder that to understand the theology of Scripture is not necessarily to embrace it.

## I

It is Bultmann's contention that by purging away every element of myth which adheres to the biblical record the essence of the gospel will remain. This essence is the *kerygma*, the truth to be preached, the irreducible core with which our modern age must be confronted. All that is incompatible with the temper and outlook of our scientific era must be jettisoned as mythological; otherwise, he maintains, we are placing a stumbling-block in the way of twentieth-century man which is not at all the real stumbling-block of the Christian gospel. In response to the inquiry whether the New Testament embodies 'a truth which is quite independent of its mythological setting' he says that, if it does, 'theology must undertake the task of stripping the Kerygma from its mythical framework'.[1] This, in brief, is Bultmann's thesis. In examining it we must first inquire what precisely he means by 'myth'.

Bultmann, as a matter of fact, is not always consistent in the significance which he assigns to the term. Sometimes he says that mythology must be abandoned. He asserts, for example, that 'the Church can re-establish communication with modern man and speak with an authentic voice only after she has reso-

[1] *Kerygma and Myth*, p. 3. London, 1953.

lutely abandoned mythology '.² But there are occasions when he says that mythology has to be interpreted rather than eliminated. In contrast to the 'older liberals', whom he accuses of having used criticism 'to *eliminate* the mythology of the New Testament' and of having thrown away 'not only the mythology but also the kerygma itself', he declares that 'our task today is to use criticism to *interpret* it'; to which he adds the remark: 'Of course, it may still be necessary to eliminate mythology here and there'.³

Here, however, any contradiction is apparent rather than real, for he is using the term in two different senses — which, from the point of view of consistency, is rather unfortunate. The mythology which has to be interpreted he defines as follows: 'Mythology is the use of imagery to express the otherworldly in terms of this world and the divine in terms of human life, the other side in terms of this side '.⁴ If *this* is mythology, then there is absolutely no hope of banishing it from the picture. There are, of course, no other terms than the terms of this world for the expression of anything whatever, concrete or abstract, in a manner which will be intelligible to man. Myth, when understood in this sense, inextricably permeates all human thought and language, for the mythological is then only a synonym for the symbolical.

But it is the other type of mythology, the type that he wishes to eliminate, with which Bultmann is preoccupied in his campaign for demythologization. This form of mythology is in the main identified with the cosmology or world-view of the New Testament which he decries as 'the cosmology of a prescientific age '.⁵ At least it may be said that Bultmann is under no illusion concerning the demand that he is making: to accept *one* mythological element renders it logically necessary to accept the whole of the New Testament. Accordingly he affirms that 'the mythical view of the world must be accepted or rejected *in its entirety* '.⁶ Acceptance of it involves, he believes, 'a sacrifice of the intellect' which can only result in 'a curious form of schizophrenia and insincerity '.⁷ And so he rejects it *in toto*.

Now, it is important that we should know just what the process of demythologization, as envisaged by Bultmann, entails. What, precisely, are we being asked to abandon? Bultmann, who is nothing if not frank in defining what, on his terms, must

---

² *op. cit.*, p. 123.
³ *op. cit.*, p. 13.
⁴ *op. cit.*, p. 10.

⁵ *op. cit.*, p. 3.
⁶ *op cit.*, p. 9 (italics mine).
⁷ *op cit.*, p. 4.

## SCRIPTURE AND MYTH

be rejected, has made it no difficult task to answer this question. The following list indicates some of the elements of the New Testament which he demands should be eliminated as mythological and unacceptable to the modern mind:
The miraculous or supernormal as a whole, as being incompatible with the modern view of the world as a closed system governed by laws which are both discernible and constant. This is a ruling concept which controls and explains the items that follow.

The pre-existence of Christ.
The virgin birth of Christ.
The sinlessness of Christ.
The deity of Christ.
The substitutionary death of Christ on the cross.
The resurrection of Christ from the dead.
The ascension of Christ into heaven.
The future return of Christ in glory.
The final judgment of the world.
The existence of spirits, good or evil.
The personality and power of the Holy Spirit.
The doctrine of the Trinity.
Death as a consequence of sin.
The doctrine of original sin.

This is, of course, a formidable list, and we shall have occasion to refer more fully to its contents in due course. The mere listing of them, however, is sufficient to demonstrate that what Bultmann demands is nothing less than a radical transformation of classical Christianity. Indeed, the reader's immediate reaction will probably be to ask whether Bultmann has not after all done what he accuses the liberal theologians of last century of doing, namely, throwing away the kerygma with the mythology. To be able to judge whether this is so, we must discover what constitutes for him the indispensable kerygma of the New Testament and what the inevitable scandal or stumbling-block of that kerygma is. He defines the kerygma for us in these terms:

> The message of the New Testament is not a *weltanschauung* which would teach the *idea* of a forgiving God, or the idea of God's grace; on the contrary, it is the proclamation of an *act* of God, by which he forgives sin . . . The New Testament proclaims that the freedom and arbitrary nature of God's action is authenticated by the fact that

he has acted decisively for all the world and for all time in the person of a concrete, historical man, *Jesus of Nazareth*. Through him everyone is addressed and asked if he is willing to hear God's message of forgiveness and grace here. In Jesus Christ the destiny of every man is decided. He is *the eschatological act of God*.[8]

In support of this statement — which, taken at its face value most Christians would have no difficulty in accepting — Bultmann cites 2 Cor. v. 17-19:

Therefore if any man be in Christ, he is a new creature: old things are passed away; behold, all things are become new. And all things are of God, who hath reconciled us to himself by Jesus Christ, and hath given to us the ministry of reconciliation; to wit, that God was in Christ, reconciling the world unto himself, not imputing their trespasses unto them; and hath committed unto us the word of reconciliation.

It is not without significance, however, that he fails to carry this quotation to its conclusion; for St. Paul goes on to declare that, as an integral element of this message of reconciliation, God made Christ, ' who knew no sin, to be sin for us; that we might be made the righteousness of God in him ' (verse 21). But because concepts of sinlessness and substitution are out of harmony with his cosmological premisses, Bultmann is unwilling to grant them a place in the kerygma — not even when they are present in so obviously kerygmatic a declaration as this.

II

What, then, does Bultmann mean when he speaks of God as having ' acted decisively for all the world and for all time in the person of a concrete, historical man, Jesus of Nazareth '? What is the nature of this decisive act of God in Jesus Christ? When Bultmann insists that ' Christian belief has its peculiar character in speaking of an *event* ', that this ' event is *Jesus Christ* ', and that ' on this event a message is based and authenticated which confronts man as *God's Word* ',[9] it becomes necessary to establish the bounds of this event, to have an understanding concerning what does and what does not belong to it. The resolution of this

---

[8] *The Understanding of Man and the World in the New Testament and in the Greek World*, in *Essays Philosophical and Theological*, p. 82.
[9] *The Crisis of Belief*, in *Essays*, p. 11.

question will lead us at the same time to a comprehension of what, according to Bultmann, constitutes the *skandalon*, the stumbling-block, which is the genuine and irreducible core of the Christian message; for event and stumbling-block will be synonymous. The stumbling-block is seen in the fact that the kerygma is not general and expansive, but particular and confined to the narrow limits of this one event; it lies, he affirms, ' in the very assertion that belief in God simply cannot and must not arise as a general human attitude, but only as a response to God's Word and that it is this *one* Word — found in the New Testament and based on the Christ-event — which is God's Word '.[10] But the full intensity of the offence of Christ has not yet been exposed. Not only is man restricted to this one Word, but ' the Christian assertion in all its offensiveness is, in fact, just this: that a relative, historical phenomenon — namely, this particular message — is God's Word '.[11] Bultmann, that is to say, views the vital content of the message, the Christ-event, not as being in itself something unique and supernormal, but as an essentially relative phenomenon belonging to the normal order of things. And since the miraculous is, for him, synonymous with the mythological, which in turn is foreign to the kerygma, we are admonished that ' modern man ', who ' *par excellence* is technological man, . . . ought not to be burdened with the mythological element in Christianity ',[12] and that the Christian redemption ' is not a miraculous supernatural event, but an historical event wrought out in time and space '.[13] The New Testament, of course, proclaims it as both miraculous and historical, but Bultmann believes that such a double viewpoint is no longer tenable in our modern world.

We find, accordingly, that the stature of Jesus of Nazareth contracts to that of a ' mere man '[14] whose person and work are denuded of every suspicion of the supernormal. It is on this mere man, this relative mortal link in the age-long chain of humanity, that the focus of the Christian *skandalon* is concentrated. The startling and arbitrary choice by God of just this ordinary individual through whom to reveal the way of redemption for all other ordinary individuals is the stumbling-block which none can avoid. Jesus of Nazareth is indeed admitted to

---

[10] *ibid.*, p. 12.   [11] *ibid.*, p. 19.
[12] *Kerygma and Myth*, p. 122.   [13] *ibid.*, p. 43.
[14] *Theology of the New Testament*, II, pp. 46, 75; cf. p. 69.

be a 'concrete figure of history' and his crucifixion an 'historical event', but this is practically all that Bultmann is prepared to state positively about Him. For the rest, the resurrection of Christ is written off as a 'definitely non-historical event', the virgin birth, the empty tomb, and the ascension as 'legends', and the doctrine that Jesus Christ is the Son of God, a pre-existent divine being, as 'mythical'.[15] These and other elements of the New Testament perspective which are regarded as legendary are brusquely (and conveniently) dismissed as 'most certainly later embellishments of the primitive tradition'.[16]

Yet the cross, though granted to be an historical event, also has to be purged of the mythology which clings to it in the New Testament. The apostolic understanding of what took place at Calvary is summarized by Bultmann in the following terms:

> The Jesus who was crucified was the pre-existent, incarnate Son of God, and as such he was without sin. He is the victim whose blood atones for our sins. He bears vicariously the sin of the world, and by enduring the punishment for sin on our behalf he delivers us from death.

A passage like this shows clearly enough that he has not misunderstood the New Testament conception of the significance of the death of Christ. He simply rejects it as no longer acceptable. Thus he adds immediately:

> This mythological interpretation is a hotch-potch of sacrificial and juridical analogies which have ceased to be tenable for us today.[17]

It is hardly likely to be a matter of dispute that, in rejecting this apostolic understanding of the cross, Bultmann has turned his back on the very heart of the Christian gospel, as it is proclaimed in the pages of the New Testament.

### III

It will be asked: What, then, is the significance and what are the effects for mankind today of the bare crucifixion of a mere man which is devoid of all supernormal accompaniments? Bultmann's answer to this is bound up with his doctrine of the continuation or extension of the Christ-event in the act of Christ-

[15] *Kerygma and Myth*, pp. 34 f.
[16] *ibid.*, p. 39.    [17] *ibid.*, p. 35.

ian preaching. We are, in fact, told that it is through and in preaching that Christ may be said to have risen from the dead and to continue as a living, challenging reality in every age. ' Belief in the resurrection and faith that Christ himself, yes God himself, speaks in the proclaimed word . . . are identical '.[18] Arguing that Christ meets us nowhere else than in the word of preaching, Bultmann reaches the conclusion that ' the faith of Easter is just this — faith in the word of preaching '.[19] And not only Christ's resurrection but also His incarnation must be understood in connection with the act of preaching; for their reference is not to past events in the experience of Jesus Christ, but to the ' eschatological ' or ' existential ' event of my own experience in the present. Thus, according to Bultmann, Christ rises again in each act of preaching, and it is in the preacher that

> the Word of God becomes incarnate. For the incarnation is likewise an eschatological event and not a datable event of the past; it is an event which is continually being re-enacted in the event of the proclamation.[20]

By the word of preaching men are confronted ' with the question whether they are willing to understand themselves as men who are crucified and risen with Christ ';[21] in it ' Christ's death-and-resurrection becomes a possibility of existence in regard to which a decision must be made '.[22] This, it may be said, is the heart of Bultmann's gospel. That it bears little resemblance to the gospel of the apostles needs no demonstration. It has the appearance, rather, of a new mysticism or psychologism with, at its very centre, a strange confusion of categories. The crucifixion, as we have seen, is granted the status of an historical event, whereas the resurrection is denied a place in the realm of historical occurrences. What, then, is this understanding of being ' crucified and risen with Christ ' of which Bultmann speaks? We are aware that the New Testament speaks in these same terms, but with this important distinction, that it does so without any confusion of categories. There we find that both the death and the resurrection of Jesus are presented with great insistence as actual historical events, and indeed that this historicity is proclaimed as the cardinal truth around which hinges the whole significance of Christian reality in its threefold aspect:

---

[18] *Theology of the New Testament*, I, p. 305.
[19] *Kerygma and Myth*, p. 41.  [20] *ibid.*, p. 209.  [21] *ibid.*, p. 42.
[22] *Theology of the New Testament*, I, p. 302.

namely, as justification, Christ died *and* rose *for me* (Rom. iv. 25, v. 6, 8) — the objective fact of the past; as sanctification, I died *and* rose *with Christ* (Rom. vi. 1 ff.) — the subjective reality of the present; and, as consummation, I too, if I die before He comes, will be raised from the dead at His appearing (1 Cor. xv. 12 ff.; 2 Cor. iv. 14, etc.) — the certain hope of the future. Bultmann, however, offers us a combination of a definitely historical event (the crucifixion) with a definitely non-historical event (the resurrection) as affording only ' a possibility of existence ', that is, a sort of formula for existential living; nor should it be overlooked that this possibility of existence concerning which we are invited to make a decision can refer to this present life only, for, like the Christ whom Bultmann proclaims, we must anticipate the historical event of our own death, but we may not look forward to an historical resurrection after death.

As for the biblical doctrine that death is the punishment of sin, we are admonished that it is ' abhorrent to naturalism and idealism, since they both regard death as a simple and necessary process of nature ',[23] and we are permitted no option but to venerate any pronouncement of these ismic deities as sacrosanct. Death then becomes the only certainty of the future, and, beyond the point of death, Christianity becomes a way without a future. Accordingly Bultmann's theology has with justice been described as ' a faith without hope '.[24]

The flight from futurity is, of course, characteristic of the existentialist outlook, and it is further emphasized in the transformation which the concept of eschatology undergoes in the perspective which Bultmann offers. In the New Testament eschatology is in large measure concerned with future, hitherto unfulfilled events, with the last things, the culmination of the history of this age. (We do not overlook the fact that there is another and complementary aspect of New Testament eschatology which is presented in the conception that we are already, since the advent of Christ, living in the last times; but in this aspect also the perspective is extended to include the ultimate boundary of these times which is expected in the second advent

---

[23] *Kerygma and Myth*, p. 7.
[24] By Emil Brunner, *Eternal Hope*, p. 214. London, 1954; though in other respects Brunner is of the opinion that ' the work of Bultmann accomplishes a necessary service for Christian theology ' (*ibid.*, p. 21 — an opinion which should not occasion surprise since the premises of Brunner's theology do not differ radically from those of Bultmann'

of Christ in glory. The element of futurity, in other words, and of final things yet to occur, is an integral element also in this aspect of New Testament eschatology.) The attention of the existentialist, however, is focused on the present, the 'now', while, apart from the expectation of death, the dimension of the future is missing from his purview.

## IV

This preoccupation with the present at the expense of the past and the future is prominent in Bultmann's thought. Dr. John Macquarrie rightly protests against his 'excessive devaluation of the objective-historical origins of Christian faith' and corresponding tendency 'to overemphasize whatever in Christian teaching is congenial to existentialist treatment'.[25] Bultmann himself has strikingly summed up his own outlook in these words:

> The Now in which the message is proclaimed is the eschatological Now . . . . The paradox of history and eschatology is that the eschatological event has happened within history and happens everywhere in preaching. That means: eschatology in a true Christian understanding of it is not the future end of history, but history is swallowed up by eschatology. Henceforth history must no longer be understood as saving history, but as profane history.[26]

In Bultmann's theology, history has indeed been swallowed up by eschatology — eschatology, that is, of his own particular existentialist brand: no truer or terser comment could have been offered than this one which he himself has given. And it is precisely *saving history* that has been engulfed. The grand perspective of saving history, embracing past, present, and future, vanishes from view: no longer may we hand on that which we have also received from the apostles, namely, that Christ died for our sins according to the Scriptures, and that He was buried, and that He was raised again on the third day according to the Scriptures, and that He appeared to the disciples (1 Cor. xv. 3-8); no longer may we rejoice in the knowledge that we have been redeemed with precious blood, as of a lamb without blemish and without spot, even the blood of Christ, who was foreknown before the foundation of the world, but was manifested at the end of

---

[25] *An Existentialist Theology*, pp. 189, 177. London, 1955.
[26] *History and Eschatology in the New Testament*, in *New Testament Studies*, Vol. I, No. I, Sept. 1954: p. 16.

the times for our sake who through Him are believers in God, who raised Him from the dead and gave Him glory (1 Pet. i. 18-21); no longer may we affirm that our citizenship is in heaven, from whence also we wait for a Saviour, the Lord Jesus Christ who shall fashion anew the body of our humiliation, that it may be conformed to the body of His glory, according to the working whereby He is able even to subdue all things unto Himself (Phil iii. 20 f.). The catharsis of demythologization alters all that, leaving us with only a man, Jesus of Nazareth, who, like all other men born into this world, lived and struggled and died: and that, as far as the past and the future are concerned, is all there is to it.

We do not, of course, dispute the presentness of the salvation occurrence in the act of preaching, in the sense that the hearer is then confronted with a challenge which is full of contemporary significance for himself in his own particular situation; nor do we deny that what Bultmann describes as a 'merely reminiscent' historical account referring to what happened in the past' would be inadequate to make the salvation-occurrence meaningful. Mere reminiscence, in any case, cannot be preaching; it is only rehearsal. To announce that Christ was born, lived, and died and even to add that He rose again and ascended into heaven is not to reproduce the proclamation of the New Testament; for a bald rehearsal of past events, however remarkable they may be, cannot have any special significance for the hearer in his own personal situation. The essence of preaching lies in the presentation of the *meaning and relevance* of the salvation-occurrence: hence the 'for us' of the apostolic preaching — 'Christ died *for us*'; He 'was delivered *for our trespasses,* and was raised *for our justification*'.[27] All that Christ came to do was for us men and for our salvation. Preaching that is truly evangelical never fails to encounter the hearer in a manner which, in its implications and demands, is fully 'existential', that is, relevant to the hearer's situation here and now.

But, if mere reminiscence is false to the New Testament, so also is Bultmann's presentation of the salvation-occurrence as a merely 'eschatological' occurrence, repeated in every act of preaching. 'The salvation-occurrence', he says, 'is eschatological occurrence just in this fact, that it does not become a fact of the past but constantly takes place anew in the present'.[28] The

[27] Rom. v. 8, iv. 25.
[28] *Theology of the New Testament,* I, p. 302.

apostolic preaching of the New Testament, however, always directs the hearer back to the one decisive historic event in which God has once for all acted on behalf of mankind. But Bultmann robs the Christ-event of its crucial uniqueness, of its once-for-allness.[29] How can it be otherwise when it is reduced to the dimension of the commonplace? He has abandoned the confident objectivity of the apostolic proclamation for a thoroughgoing subjectivism. God-in-action is limited to the 'eschatological' now of the individual's response. Indeed, God-in-action is confined to the narrow sphere of man-in-action.

The excessively subjective character of Bultmann's position is further seen in his treatment of the New Testament assertions of the deity of Christ. His unsuccessful attempt to limit such texts to what he regards as the 'deutero-pauline' literature need not detain us here, for, since the doctrine of the deity of Christ, apart from being explicitly stated in a number of passages, is implicit and fundamental throughout the New Testament and has been maintained by the universal Church in every age, it remains a question which he also has to face. The answer he offers is that 'pronouncements about Jesus' divinity or deity are not, in fact, pronouncements of his nature but seek to give expression to his significance'[30]; that is to say, they do not affirm an objective ontological fact, the essential Godhead of Jesus, but represent an existential value-judgment, subjectively made by the individual at a particular moment. By way of illustration it is suggested that the declaration of John vi. 69 ('And we believe and are sure that thou art that Christ, the Son of the living God') should be understood 'quite simply' (!) as 'just a confession of significance for the "moment" in which it was uttered, and not a dogmatic pronouncement.'[31] In other words, *I* am the centre of reference, not, or no longer, Christ. Truth must be equated with subjectivity and subjectivity with truth, with the result that a Christological pronouncement should not be received as a statement about Christ, but interpreted as a 'pronouncement about me'. As values should now be measured by the existential yardstick, no more should I be so objective as to say that Christ helps me because He is God's Son, but rather that He is God's Son because He helps me.[32]

[29] Cf. Brunner's criticisms in this connection: *The Christian Doctrine of Creation and Redemption* (Dogmatics Vol. II), p. 268. London 1952.
[30] *The Christological Confession of the World Council of Churches*, in *Essays*, 280.
[31] *ibid.* [32] *ibid.*

Here, once again, we are face to face with an extreme form of subjectivism, involving a complete reversal of the Christological perspective of the New Testament. This being so, it is scarcely remarkable to find the Chalcedonian definition of the person of Christ dismissed as 'now impossible for our thought'. Revelation, so far from being an objective reality, is confined to ' an event in the present ', to the individualistic illuminism of the ' moment '[33], and the only history which is admitted as truly significant is that which occurs at this locus of the moment of encounter.   ' The reality of my existence ', writes Bultmann, ' . . . is actually real only in the "moment", in the question involved in the " moment " and in the decision called for by the " moment " '.[34]   There is no doubt that in the New Testament the personal response of the individual to the reality which meets him in preaching occupies a most important place; but Bultmann expounds ' true history ' entirely in terms of ' the actual living of men ',[35] that is, in terms of the present and of personal encounter, and not at all in terms of a succession of events or acts of the past, which is regarded as something outside of and therefore unreal to the individual.

According to this existential understanding of history, the only true history for each individual is his own history; being unable to detach himself from his own personal setting, the individual cannot make himself the subject over against whom history stands as an object, for he is fully and inescapably involved in existence, *his* existence, and thus is himself the centre of the only history which can have any meaning for him — his own history. And so each man's understanding of himself becomes the only valid understanding of history. When, therefore, Bultmann affirms that ' the true reality for biblical thought is *history* ', it would be a mistake to conclude that he is referring to the commonly accepted ' historical facts ' of Christianity. His meaning becomes apparent when he explains that

> inquiry into truth is for the biblical man one into the significance of the ' moment ' that confronts him,

and again that

> the real life of man . . . develops in the sphere of what is individua

---

[33] *op. cit.*, pp. 286 ff.
[34] *The Crisis in Belief*, in *Essays*, p. 8.
[35] *Theology of the New Testament*, I, p. 305.

— of contingent encounters. In his decision at a given moment . . lies the attainment or the loss of his real being.[36]

## V

In Bultmann's view, not only the whole natural order, but also, within it, the microcosm of human personality, is a closed system functioning in accordance with its own fixed laws, which exclude the possibility of interference 'from above'.[37] The circle of nature is closed and impermeable. In justification of this view the authority of 'modern science' is invoked, and as such it is a view which is founded upon the assumption of the autonomy of man as a rational being. Human reason is regarded as competent to assign the bounds of all possibility; and yet it is incompetent to declare the shape of things to come, for while all things operate in accordance with natural laws, these laws themselves are subject to no control but operate in a vacuum of unpredictable chance. They are just 'there', like the walls of an impregnable fortress which cannot be penetrated from without, but within which anything may happen. In short, this is a position in which law and chance are correlatives, and that means that reason and unreason are correlatives.

A position like this, hopelessly involved in contradictions, is of course very different from the position of Scripture, which teaches that all things are at all times under the absolute control of Almighty God and are directed by Him in conformity with His eternal purposes. This applies to the future just as much as to the past — indeed, if it did not apply to the future it would be a meaningless doctrine. Man, it is true, does not know what the morrow will bring forth; *but God does*, and the biblical Christian is a man who, so far from being restricted in his apprehension of truth to the contingent encounters of the moment, has perfect confidence, as he faces his future, that nothing will be able to frustrate God's plan for him and for the world. He is assured that the future is not governed by chance, that it is not for God the realm of mystery and the unknown, and therefore that his God is not bound by the thongs of unpredictable possibility and contingency.

But not so Bultmann's Christian man: for him, chance and uncertainty reign supreme as he faces his future, and accordingly

[36] *Adam, Where art Thou?*, in *Essays*, pp. 124 f. *Cf.* also F. Gogarten: *Demythologizing and History*. London 1955.
[37] V. *Kerygma and Myth*, p. 7.

the possibility of reality is tied to the fleeting moment of the present. The man who wishes all things to be subject to the rational and systematic control of his intellect is confronted with the future as with a monstrous unorganized spectre which, because it is at the mercy of the irrational forces of chance and contingency, it is beyond his powers to control or predict. And the ultimate and crushing irrationality is that of death — *his* death (for this much he does know about his future) — in which the dissolution of all his rational faculties takes place. Of course, as the irrational phantom of the future moves into his past man will rationalize it; but the monster of the unknown and the uncertain still looms before him: he can never rid himself of his future, not even in the hour of death — indeed, least of all then, for it is then that the question of the future assumes its most dreadful proportions. The future is a constant reminder to him of his finiteness, his insufficiency, his fallenness. It is the shadow of chaos hanging darkly over his neatly interpreted cosmos; for while he will tell you what cannot possibly come to pass, he cannot possibly tell you what will come to pass.

The salvation of man, according to Bultmann, lies in 'openness' to the future, in his being 'receptive to the future which is making itself accessible in what confronts me in the "now"'.[38] Again, freedom is defined as 'nothing else than being open for the genuine future, letting one's self be determined by the future'.[39] Man, we are told, 'falls a prey to nothingness and death in cutting himself off from the future in dread'; indeed, 'the real crux of sin' is located in 'the dread of the man who is unwilling to surrender to what is mystery to him'[40] whereas God's way of salvation is declared in the forgiveness of sin, which, says Bultmann,

> means simply the obliteration of man's past, and taking him to be what he is not — the man of the future; it means relieving him of dread and thereby making him free for the future.[41]

This, however, is still a gospel of uncertainty, and, as such it is not the gospel of the New Testament which is one of assurance for the future and for ever. It is uncertain because it is constructed round an illusory concept, for if the present is the

[38] *The Understanding of Man*, etc., *ut sup.*, p. 80.
[39] *Theology of the New Testament*, I, p. 335.
[40] *The Understanding of Man*, etc., *ut sup.*, p. 81.
[41] *ibid.*, p. 85.

moment at which the future moves into the sphere of existential reality, it is also the moment, the point without dimension, at which the future becomes the past, the moment, that is, at which the future ceases to be future and becomes its opposite. It is a point not of security, but of insecurity. For Bultmann, accordingly, Christian faith and knowledge are at best but 'momentary', constantly in need of renewal and dependent on repeated decision.[42] Again, for him, insecurity is 'what characterizes the real nature of human existence', and it is out of the situation of the moment, which is the point where man's real existence finds expression in decision, that 'his insecurity breaks in on him'.[43] All this is of a piece with Kierkegaard's doctrine that 'truth is subjectivity' and that it, together with faith, is therefore associated with 'objective uncertainty'.[44] So also with Bultmann truth is subjectivity and may not be objectified; it is limited to the moment of personal encounter, that point at which man appears to meet his future, and therefore the point at which he hopes somehow to resolve the conflict between the rational and the irrational that destroys both his peace of heart and the consistency of his understanding of things.

## VI

'All our thinking today', declares Bultmann, 'is shaped . . . by modern science.' 'Now that the forces and laws of nature have been discovered' the miracles of the New Testament 'have ceased to be miraculous'; it is 'impossible . . . to believe in the New Testament world of daemons and spirits'; the 'mythical escatology' is 'untenable', and so 'we can no longer look for the return of the Son of Man on the clouds of heaven or hope that the faithful will meet in the air'; and, thanks to 'modern man's understanding of himself', it can now be asserted that human nature is 'a self-subsistent unity immune from the interference of supernatural powers'.[45] But what is this intangible impersonal something called 'modern science' whose authority Bultmann finds so compelling? It is no more satisfactory an entity than Kierkegaard discovered 'speculative philosophy' to

[42] *Cf. Humanism and Christianity*, in *Essays*, p. 154, and *The Crisis in Belief, ibid.*, pp. 5, 15.
[43] *The Crisis in Belief, ut sup.*, p. 8.
[44] *Cf.* S. Kierkegaard: *Concluding Unscientific Postscript*, pp. 53, 82, 540, etc. Princeton, 1944.
[45] *Kerygma and Myth*, pp. 3 ff.

be in his day. We may well substitute the former for the latter and (with one further slight adaptation) say in Kierkegaard's words: 'It seems strange that people are always talking of modern science as if it were a man, or as if a man were modern science. It is modern science that does everything, that understands everything, and so forth. The scientist, on the other hand, has become too objective to talk about himself; he does not say that he understands everything, but that modern science does, and that he makes this affirmation about modern science'.[46]

It is by no means the case, despite the impression that Bultmann gives, that the totality of modern scientists have formed the judgment that the world of nature is a closed system in which there is no room for the miraculous or the inexplicable. On the contrary, the tendency of modern scientific theory and research is to view nature as more 'open' than ever. Bultmann's confident assertions concerning modern science are scarcely in harmony with the temper of scientific thought of the present day; it would be nearer the mark to suggest, with respect, that they reflect the popular notions of so-called 'modern science' at the time of his youth. Macquarrie is not being unjust when he writes of Bultmann:

> He is still obsessed with the pseudo-scientific view of a closed universe that was popular half a century ago, and anything which does not fit into that tacitly assumed world-picture is, in his view, not acceptable to the modern mind and assigned to the realm of myth.[47]

In any case, each succeeding generation is tempted afresh to regard the science of its day as having spoken the final word and therefore as being in a sense static: whereas true science is always in a state of transition: however great its advances, it never ceases to be on the threshold of new discoveries which may well be of a revolutionary character. Science that is 'modern' today will be outmoded tomorrow.

The fallacy of thinking that theological truth must constantly undergo accommodation to the dogmas of science, as though the latter were something settled and ultimate, is aptly illustrated when it is remembered that until recently we were solemnly assured that 'modern science' had made it impossible to believe any longer in a catastrophic end of the world, such as is anticipated in the Bible. Today, however, as a result of the startling

[46] *Concluding Unscientific Postscript*, p. 50.
[47] *op cit.*, p. 168.

advances in atomic physics and nuclear fission, with all the catastrophic potentialities involved, we are blandly told that modern science permits us to return to this belief which a short while ago was dismissed as absurdly unscientific. Theologians therefore who fall into line behind the science of the day have had to perform a complete *volte face*. Thus Brunner instructs us:

> What until recently seemed to be only the apocalyptic fantasies of the Christian faith has today entered the sphere of the soberest scientific calculations: the sudden end of human history . . . This thought has ceased to be absurd, i.e. to be such that a man educated in modern scientific knowledge would have to give it up.[48]

It is, of course, the scientist's task to seek to achieve an understanding of the processes of nature and to explain the relationship between the facts that are discovered. But, while the *method* of science is properly *a posteriori*, it is important to remember that scientific activity proceeds, indeed builds, upon the assumption — itself an *a priori* premiss — that the natural realm is an ordered system governed by laws which it is the aim of the scientist to discover. The scientist *presupposes* that one fact will lead on logically to another. This is a very necessary assumption, for unless the facts of the universe are coherent and interrelated with each other all meaningful investigation of natural phenomena becomes an impossibility. To suggest that each fact is solitary and independent of other facts would be to suggest that nothing in the world has any meaning at all; for facts in isolation cease to be facts: they are then just the symbols of chaos. For science to be even a possibility the presupposition that nature is a *universe*, a co-ordinated whole, is essential. The *a posteriori* method must construct its scientific edifice upon this *a priori* foundation.

Yet this presupposition of the coherence of the natural order is an unpremeditated assumption; it is a *datum* which is native to man. Thus the scientist who professes such objectivity and openness of mind that he is willing to follow the facts wherever they may lead him, still *premises* that the facts will lead him somewhere. For the truth is that every man *knows*, inwardly and constitutionally, that the world is a cosmos and not a chaos; and he knows, further, that the reason for this is that all things, himself included, have been created in accordance with the design and purpose of Almighty God. This knowledge is both

[48] *Eternal Hope*, p. 127.

innate and revealed.

It is *innate* knowledge because man by virtue of his creaturehood sustains within his very being an inescapable and constitutive relationship both to the Creator and to the rest of creation which makes him instinctively aware of the order and consistency of God's world. Not to know this is not to know oneself. It is the very heart of human existence and understanding. To know the world as the handiwork of God is entirely natural to him who has been created in the image of God.

It is *revealed* knowledge because wherever man turns it confronts him in his cosmic environment. All things are eloquent of this fundamental truth — as the psalmist sang many hundreds of years ago: 'The heavens declare the glory of God; and the firmament sheweth his handywork. Day unto day uttereth speech, and night unto night sheweth knowledge. There is no speech nor language; their voice is not heard. Their line is gone out through all the earth, and their words to the end of the world' (Ps. xix. 1-4). St. Paul speaks to the same effect when he affirms that the invisible things of God, even His eternal power and godhead, are clearly seen from the creation of the world, being perceived from the things that have been created: with the consequence that men are without excuse when they deny the sovereign rights of the Creator and withhold from Him their worship and homage (Rom. i. 20 ff.). This general revelation is so obvious that no man can fail to see it. No man, scientist or otherwise, can plead ignorance of the truth which it displays, for, once again, by virtue of his own creation in the image of God, it is impossible for him to be unaware of the witness of the Creator's omnipotence and sovereignty which the whole created realm constantly presents to his gaze.

And yet it is precisely this ever-present revelation that fallen man is unwilling to acknowledge. He allows sin to blind him to its pure light and wickedly expresses his sinfulness and rebellion by holding down or suppressing the truth in unrighteousness (Rom. i. 18). Indeed, in this passage (Rom. i. 18 ff.) the apostle sums up the whole story of human sin and depravity: while '*knowing* God', he says, men 'glorified him not as God neither gave thanks'; instead they 'became vain in their own reasonings', with the result that 'their foolish heart was darkened'. Preoccupation with human wisdom and philosophy leads men to expend their intellectual and spiritual energies on the interminable 'quest for truth' when all the time the truth is staring them in the face, as plain as noonday. '*Professing themselves to be wise, they became fools*' says St. Paul — could anything expose more starkly the extreme folly and futility of sin? In brief, what man has done is to exchange the truth of God for a lie and to worship and serve the creature rather than the Creator (verse 25). This is true not merely of the idolatry of heathenism, but of the anthropocentrism of civilization.

## VII

The grotesqueness of the position of unregenerate man is further seen in that, while he wishes to do without the truth of the absolute sovereignty of God as evidenced by creation, yet it is a truth which he is quite unable to do without since it is the essential foundation of his own and of all existence. God as Creator is the ground both of his existence as a human being and of the existence of the whole created order, of which he is but a part. But God as Creator is also the ground of all knowledge. The orderliness of creation, as revelatory of the mind of God, is the essential framework for man's function as a rational being. Were the universe marked by incoherence (and if it were we should be unable even to form the concepts of coherence and incoherence or to engage in logical thought and communication), and were it not possible to proceed from one fact to another, the scientist would have no method and the thinker would have no system. In other words, all being and all knowledge are inevitably related to God who, as Creator of all things, is the sole ground of all possibility and all rationality.

The basic contradiction at the root of the thinking of unregenerate man consists simply in this: that alongside the principle of rationality, which is a necessity for all logical procedure, he introduces a principle of irrationality; that is to say, he *knows* the truth about the eternal power and godhead of the Creator, and that all things are ordered in accordance with the plan and will of the sovereign Deity — the truth which alone makes possible a rational and scientific understanding of the world — and yet at the same time he irrationally *suppresses* this truth, he will not have God to rule over him, but wishes to interpret the facts of the universe in terms of a philosophy which is autocentric instead of theocentric, and which therefore glorifies man rather than God. This is the height of irrationality. His highest faculties are crippled by this contradiction at the heart of his being. Hence the frustration of all men's 'systems' of philosophical wisdom, which, impressive though they may appear to be, yet because of the inherent contradiction in his thinking not only are stamped with frailty and inconsistency, but also and for this reason are destructive of one another.

But scientific activity is also dependent on another principle, which must not be overlooked. This principle too is assumed *a priori*, instinctively taken for granted, even by the most devotedly ' objective ' investigator. It is, namely, that of the ability of the higher to intervene in the affairs of the lower. Without this faculty there could, again, be no science, for scientific activity is precisely this principle in operation. Thanks to this faculty, man is able increasingly to turn the resources of the world to his own use and to harness the forces of nature for the benefit (or destruction) of his race; he is able, that is, to be scientific man.

This consideration in itself is sufficient to demonstrate that while he recognizes that the realm of nature, being informed by a harmony of laws and relationships, is one of order and not chaos man *knows* that it is not a hermetically 'closed' system. His faculty of intervention, whereby he is able to interrupt, intensify, and within measure control the potencies of his world, is proof sufficient that there is an aspect of the natural order that is essentially ' open '. It affords further clear evidence of the image of God in which man was created; for it is by virtue of his creation in the image of God that he possesses and exercises this power. As the crown of God's handiwork, he has been commanded to subdue and have dominion over the rest of the created order (Gn. i. 26-28). Yet, once again, unregenerate man in his rational conquest of nature irrationally suppresses the knowledge of the truth: he denies that the Creator, who is the Highest (Lk. i. 32), is able to intervene in His own creation! He declares that the system is closed to its Maker! Constitutive though it is of his being and his knowledge, he does not wish to be reminded that he bears the image of God and so he invents the self-deception of his own ultimacy. This grossly irrational attitude is doubtless, at its roots, dictated by the fear of judgment to come: a God who is impotent to intervene in the affairs of this world is impotent also to intervene in final judgment.

The record of Holy Scripture is, of course, from beginning to end, a witness to the intervention and overruling of Almighty God in the affairs of men in accordance with His purposes. In the biblical purview, therefore, the plan of God is manifested not only in the natural order but also in the development of history. This means that, as the Lord of creation, God is also the Lord of the future, and as such the Lord of salvation and of judgment. To assert this, however, is not to exclude secondary causes or to deny the responsibility of man. Jesus Christ, to take the supreme example, was certainly shamefully 'crucified and slain by the hands of wicked men' (the secondary cause), but at the same time He was 'delivered up by the determinate counsel and foreknowledge of God' (the primary cause) (Acts ii. 23; *cf.* Jn. x. 17 f.). The agents of wickedness cannot frustrate the purposes of God which move on majestically to their destined fulfilment in redemption and in judgment; yet they do not therefore cease to be the responsible agents of wickedness. The God of the Bible is not pathetically excluded from a universe that is closed to His intervention, nor is He a helpless watcher of events over which He has no control. For Him who knows the end from the beginning, and who 'works all things according to the counsel of his will' (Eph. i. 11), the future is not a dimension of unpredictable contingency.

The God of the Scriptures, then, is the ground not only of all being but also of all knowledge. It is a fallacy characteristic of fallen mankind to believe that the question of knowledge can be divorced from the question of being. This is plainly illustrated in the account of the fall (Gn. iii). Eve had no doubts about the being of God, but she succumbed to the temptation to doubt His knowledge. Concerning the tree of the knowledge of good and evil, God had said: 'In the day that thou eatest thereof thou shalt surely die'; but Satan contradicted this word of God. He suggested, in effect, that there were sources of knowledge other than God Himself and that it was not necessary to regard the word of God as authoritative. He insinuated that no one, not even God, can say beforehand what is going to happen, since the future is a haze of unformed contingent possibilities. Therefore the woman must be open to receive knowledge from any and every quarter, to put away the dread of the future, and to realize her authentic being in her own subjective decision of the moment with which she is confronted. Surrounded though she was by the unmistakable evidences of the Creator's eternal power and godhead, and, moreover, enlightened by the revelation of a special word from His mouth, she who bore His image yet turned her back on the light and wilfully chose the road of self-assertion and disobedience which led inevitably to ruin. Previously she had had the knowledge of good alone, the pure good of God's benevolence; now she has the knowledge of good *and evil*, which, as the account shows, is accompanied by the knowledge of guilt and judgment.

But Eve's decision concerning the knowledge of God also implied a decision concerning the being of God. Had she considered His being as the Sovereign Designer and Creator of herself and of all that exists, she could never have doubted that His knowledge must be absolute and constitutive of the knowledge of all His creatures. But in sitting in judgment on God's knowledge she in effect sat in judgment upon His being, thereby implying that it must be on a level with, or at any rate only relatively and not absolutely different from, her own being. She attempted to arrogate to herself the authority which rightly and uniquely belongs to God.[49]

## VIII

If the being of God is *not* such as the Bible declares it to be then the one we worship is an idol, a no-god, of our own fabrication. If the being of God *is* such as the Bible declares it to be, then it is obvious that we cannot know anything truly and accurately except in so far as our knowledge is a reflection of the knowledge of Him who alone is the eternal, omniscient, and self-sufficient Source and Sovereign of all. Before such a God we can join in the apostle's doxology: ' O the depth of the riches both of the wisdom and knowledge of God! . . . For of him, and through him, and to him, are all things: to whom be glory for ever. Amen ' (Rom. xi. 33-36). Even though, in the nature of the case, our knowledge must be partial compared with the completeness and ultimacy of God's knowledge, yet that does not mean that our knowledge cannot be correct knowledge.

Here the question of revelation is involved. Revelation *from* God alone ensures the reliability and adequacy for man's requirements of the truth imparted, whether it be the general and as it were silent revelation which confronts man in the natural realm, or the special, verbal revelation of Holy Scripture the function of which is to give knowledge of God's provision for man's salvation. For divine revelation is necessarily authoritative; indeed, in the ultimate issue, there can be but one source of authority: God Himself. The creature knows full well that every utterance and revelation coming from the Creator must

---

[49] *Cf.* Cornelius Van Til: *The Defense of the Faith*, pp. 50 ff., 135 f. Philadelphia, 1955.

be absolutely authoritative. But the sinfulness of man ever asserts itself by the denial of the word, that is, the knowledge, of God. Sinful man ever wishes to make himself the centre of authority, the author of knowledge, and the arbiter of what is possible. The issue, in its simplest terms, revolves round the question whether we are to let God be God or man be God. Sinful man, as in the blindness of his pride he opposes his authority to that of God's revelation, is still fatally beguiled by the satanic promise, ' Ye shall be as God, knowing good and evil '. Yet it should be noticed that even these words of temptation betray the realization that knowledge and being are not independent of each other: to be as God is to know as God.

What Bultmann has done is, in one word, to pose once again the all-important question of authority. But in doing so he has fallen into the primeval error of imagining that the question of knowledge may be treated in separation from that of being. Nowhere does he seek to call into question the being of God; but this, so far from being a mark of merit, is in fact *the crucial inconsistency* in his system. For throughout, by setting up the knowledge of ' modern man ' and ' modern science ' as determinative of what is and what is not possible in our world, he proclaims that the knowledge of man is authoritative and thereby pronounces against the knowledge and the authority of God. That means that in effect, though not in intention, he pronounces against the being of God. It is hardly surprising that in his writings God has the appearance of being an unexplained ' foreign body '. Can he not see that the logic of his own position cries out for him to take the one last step of declaring ' God ' to be the ultimate myth that has to be eliminated?

In eliminating every element of the miraculous and the supernormal Bultmann has carried out a thoroughgoing ' kenosis ' of Scripture. It is important to remember, however, that, although it is now common to speak of the ' natural ' and the ' supernatural ' as though they belonged to two opposite categories, Scripture knows of no such cleavage. The reason for this is that the biblical perspective is not anthropocentric but consistently theocentric. According to the Bible, all things are of God, whether they be miracles or normal natural phenomena. Thus all things come within one and the same category, for they are all the works of Almighty God. The standard whereby things are to be judged is seen not in the regular cycle of natural law, but in the very character of God Himself. As the Creator, Sustainer, and Governor of the world, everything that

He does excites wonder and admiration, whether it be the ordered harmony of the universe or some supernormal occurrence displaying His mercy or judgment. All things testify to God's perfection and sovereignty, from the humble flower in the field (Solomon in all his glory was not arrayed like one of these) to the majestic constellations, from the despised sparrow to the marvel of man's constitution. Nothing is commonplace or unimpressive; the whole universe bears the stamp of God's supreme and exuberant creativity, and the miraculous, though supernormal as perceived by man, is of a piece with the normal. The miraculous is concentrated in three great events or interventions: *creation*, whereby this whole amazing universe was brought into being by the Word of God; secondly, *redemption*, involving the incarnation, death, resurrection, and ascension of Christ, whereby man, and with him the world, is rescued from the consequences of his sin; and thirdly, *consummation*, whereby, at Christ's second coming, God's work of mercy and judgment will be brought to completion and the new earth wherein righteousness dwells will be introduced. All other miraculous interventions are subservient to God's purposes in creation, redemption, and judgment.

## IX

This all-embracing biblical perspective, which ascribes all things to the power and wisdom of God, is also the only genuinely Christian perspective. It alone provides a full and consistent explanation of all the facts of man and the world. No other explanation is (nor can be) free from incapacitating contradictions. Scripture is addressed to man as a rational being, but it is not subject to the judgment of human reason; for it must not be forgotten that it is also addressed to man *as a sinner*, whose mind has been so darkened by sin that he would like to think that he is the autonomous and self-sufficient judge of all truth. The scriptural revelation, indeed, is an integral element in the redemptive purposes of God's grace, for it is a particular function of Holy Scripture to make man, foolish lost man, ' wise unto salvation through faith which is in Christ Jesus ' (2 Tim iii. 15). The authority of Scripture therefore is a *dynamic* authority, the authority of the Word of God, who is Himself the sole and supreme source of all authority. That is why the word of Scripture is a creative, or re-creative, word of authority from God to man: presenting the truth to man's mind and exposing his state as a sinner before God, it testifies to Him who is God's supreme and final Word to man, our Lord and Saviour Jesus Christ.

To attempt to demonstrate the authority of Scripture as the Word of God by reason or tradition or probability is not only a vain occupation but subversive of the very authority claimed for Scripture, for then human judgment, in the form of reason, tradition, probability, and so on, is set up as an authority superior to that of divine revelation, to which the latter must submit. To do this is in effect to deny the supremacy of Holy Scripture as the Word of God. This does not mean, however, that the Christian is invited to take a leap in the dark where the Bible is concerned — on the contrary, for, firstly, Scripture, as God's revelation, is clear and luminous and self-authenticating, and secondly, the believer has an entirely adequate and conclusive witness to Scripture as the authoritative revelation of God in the Holy Spirit who confirms it as the Word of God to his heart. The internal testimony of the Holy Spirit, which the Reformers stressed, is conclusive, and it is at the same time a testimony that is both objective (as being that of the Holy Spirit) and subjective (as being within the believer's own heart).

If the Bible is not the authoritative Word of God, but just a fortuitous human document representing a localized history of man's feeling after the numinous, its authority can at best be no more than that of probability; man is then cast adrift upon the boundless ocean of uncertainty, his quest for final truth is condemned to endless frustration on the rational-irrational rise and fall of the waves of subjectivity and chance, and he must content himself with the God of philosophical surmise and speculation who becomes an unknown ' being beyond ' and who may and equally may not exist somewhere over the furthest horizon of man's thought — a being at the unexplored circumference of possibility and not by any means at the centre of reality. Such a being bears no relation to the Triune God, revealing Himself in His world as Creator, Redeemer, and Judge, the knowledge of whom is communicated by Scripture alone. Such a being is a nonentity unable to utter any word of authority, let alone control all things in accordance with the power and purpose of His will.

Yet it is to this puny stature that God seems to have been reduced in the theology of Rudolf Bultmann; and this can be explained only as the consequence of his setting up of modern man's understanding of himself and the world as authoritative.

In adopting this anthropocentric position he has failed to take into account the fact that the natural man wilfully suppresses the truth about God and His creation. Indeed, it seems that Bultmann's own thinking is conformed to that of the natural man — though in saying this we are not presuming to pass judgment on his spiritual condition: it is God alone who sees the heart, and we realize that it is regettably possible for regenerate man to allow his thinking to be influenced, if not controlled, by the thinking of unregenerate man. Nor are we unappreciative of the fact that Bultmann has been impelled by the commendable desire to make the Christian message intelligible and relevant to modern man. He has, however, permitted his zeal to carry him to such extremes that the Christian message has been robbed of its essential content. The relevance of the gospel to his condition will not become apparent to modern man as the result of the demythologization of Scripture, for the things of God and of Christ are foolishness to him and his heart is closed against them (1 Cor. ii. 14). It is only the Holy Spirit testifying unitedly with Holy Scripture to the saving Person and work of Jesus Christ, who can dispel the darkness of unbelief and cause the sinner to open his heart to the gospel as alone adequate to his needs. The Holy Spirit and Holy Scripture together point to the Lamb of God who bears away the sin of the world, to Him who is the *Logos*, the fount of all rationality and significance, ' in whom are hid all the treasures of wisdom and knowledge ' (Col. ii. 3).